RANDY
SIMMONS

Christian Communications
P.O. Box 150
Nashville, TN 37202

Published by Christian Communications
A Division of Gospel Advocate Co.
P.O. Box 150, Nashville, TN 37202

ISBN 0-89225-299-5

Contents

Lesson 1

"Dating Is Preparation for Marriage"

Dating is a normal part of life. It plays an important role in the decision-making process a young person goes through in choosing a life-time partner. Simply put, "You marry whom you date." So dating affects every segment of your life, both present and future.

Dating is not just a casual procedure. It is preparation for marriage, always. Of course, you don't marry *every* person that you date, but *you are going to marry some person you date*. Every date is a potential mate.

Dating should never be taken lightly. It should always be approached seriously. Many of the broken marriages and divided families we see today are the result of a careless attitude toward dating. Since dating is preparation for marriage, poor preparation for our dating life can lead to a lifetime of unhappiness and misery.

With this in mind, let's discuss the purposes of dating:

1. Dating helps you get to know people of the opposite sex;
2. In dating, you make contacts and abiding friendships;

3. Dating brings tolerance and understanding of the opposite sex;
4. Dating satisfies the normal instinct of personality and the enjoyment of fellowship;
5. Dating helps you discover and control your emotions;
6. No other entrance into marriage is acceptable in our society. Therefore, dating is preparation for marriage.

In your dating life, you need to keep these purposes of dating firmly in mind. You need a healthy concept of what dating is all about, if you are to have a truly successful dating life and marriage to follow.

You have been given six purposes of dating. Now let me tell what dating is not (no matter what the world tells you):

1. Dating is not the way for a boy to get what he wants from a girl. In case he doesn't know what he wants, the world tells him that, too, through movies, TV, music, and cheap talk. It tells him he wants sex. That is a phony, anti-Christian message. Sex is not love; it is not even fellowship. In fact, in the truest sense, sex is not something you do, it is something you are.
2. Dating is not the way for a girl to get what she wants from a boy. The world tells her she must get everything out of the boy she can—going to nice places, getting him to spend a lot of money on her.

In both cases, one person is just *using* the other. These are the lies about dating that the world feeds teenagers today. These lies are tearing homes apart almost as fast as they can be put together.

Let me share with you what I believe are appropriate standards for dating. Certainly these are not all the

You ARE going to marry some person you date...

standards a Christian should consider in dating, but they provide us a good starting point:

1. *Date other Christians.* This is a hard rule for young Christians to live by, but it is important. The world (and you) can come up with all kinds of reasons why you should date non-Christians: "He (or she) is not a Christian but a nice person"; or, "He (or she) is more moral than most of the hypocritical Christians I know"; or, "I think I can influence him (or her) to become a Christian". When you hear these rationalizations about dating a non-Christian,

be on guard. There are several good reasons for not dating non-Christians:

a. God doesn't want you to (there is evidence of this from both the Old and New Testaments).

b. A marriage plagued by religious differences is a serious problem (5th leading cause of divorce).

c. What about children? Where will they go? Will they be split from mother or father, religiously speaking?

d. What if the other person influences you more than you influence them? Someone says, "But there are people who have led their partners to Heaven." That is true. But far more Christian partners have been led to Hell! I honestly believe you will have a much happier dating life if you commit yourself to dating other Christians.

2. *Pre-determine to avoid excessive physical involvement.* You notice I said "excessive." The main danger is that it can lead to premarital sex and the many problems it can cause (pregnancy, disease, feelings of uncleaness, a bad reputation, turn-off to future marriage partners, guilt feelings for a lifetime, sinning against God's will). If you pre-determine to limit your physical involvement in dating, it can save you a lifetime of heartache and emotional problems.

3. *Break off any relationship that violates God-given principles and standards.* Better to break it off now than during engagement, or worse yet marriage! If you can't get along now, you can forget getting along later when problems will get *much* worse. And they will get worse fast when you know you are violating God's will and your own principles, as your conscience plagues you almost constantly.

Other standards are important, but these are surely the main three. Since dating is preparation for marriage, perhaps we should spend some time discussing how to make the most of marriage.

Marriages are falling apart all over our land. Over 50 percent of all marriages in the United States are now ending in divorce. Divorce plagues not only the marriage partners but also children, parents, friends and fellow Christians.

Something must be done about divorce. I subscribe to the age-old adage, "An ounce of prevention is worth a pound of cure." So, in this lesson, we want to focus on how to make the most of marriage, in the hopes that if you learn these truths *before* marrying, your marriage may prosper and be successful.

The origin of marriage comes from God Himself, who performed the first wedding in the Garden of Eden (Genesis 2:18-24). After making man, God saw that "it is not good that man should be alone; I will make a help meet for him" (Genesis 2:18). So, God made the kind of man who needed a wife or a life companion. And He made Eve because she was needed and because she would fit in with the normal and happy life of Adam. Thus, marriage was instituted by God and is blessed by God.

Why should people marry? What is the benefit of marriage? What are the purposes of marriage? Let me list a few of the purposes:

1. *Marriage provides companionship and fellowship.* Marriage is intended of God to be the answer for a lonely heart and to supply love, fellowship, comfort, sharing and joy. Loneliness is not good, and marriage satisfies the natural need for companionship.

2. *Marriage is to avoid fornication and give a normal outlet for the release of sexual feelings and desires.* God created man and woman with certain physical desires and attractions for one another. Marriage fulfills these desires in the way God planned (Hebrews 13:4). A man needs a woman and a woman needs a man, physically speaking. There is nothing dirty or wrong with these needs being fulfilled in the marriage bond. In fact, it is totally right, as a means of expressing deep love for one another. Kept within the boundaries of the marriage bond, this biological attraction is one of the purposes of marriage. On the other hand, fornication is expressly forbidden throughout the

There are several good reasons for not dating non-Christians.

Scriptures and Paul indicates in 1 Corinthians 7:1-2, 9 that marriage helps people avoid fornication and the lusts of the flesh.

3. *Another obvious purpose of marriage is to propagate the human race, to bear children* (Genesis 1:28). Women were made with the physical ability to bear children and, I believe, with a maternal instinct. Men were made to shoulder responsibility as a husband and father.

4. *Marriage is important in the total picture of a home.* We must continue to bear children to exist . . . and children need a mother, father and home. So one of the purposes for marriage is the management of a home and the training of children.

5. *Of course, people also marry for love.* In fact, people should not marry who do not love each other deeply. I might add that the kind of love that should lead to marriage is emotional, spiritual and mental as well as physical.

Now that we have looked closely at some of the purposes of marriage, let's notice some things that should delay marriage:

1. *One should wait until old enough to marry.* This age distinction may vary from person to person. Actual statistics show that teenage marriages fail twice as often as other marriages. So, age must be an important factor. There is no reason to rush marriage. Wait until you know each other better; wait until you are more mature and know what you want for life.

2. *One should wait for true love.* Physical attraction, no matter how strong, is not necessarily love. Some marriages are no more than an attempt to live together at the physical level. There is little sharing of spiritual things, motives, goals, or plans for the future. The only thing shared is a bedroom. This will not work!

There must be genuine love or marriage should be delayed.

3. *One should wait until he/she knows the other person extremely well.* Short engagements are dangerous and rarely succeed. The longer you are around someone, the better you are able to evaluate their *entire* character and not just the personality trait that may have swept you off your feet!

4. *One should wait until finances are under control.* Especially in our tough economic age, it is essential to have a solid financial base and support before entering marriage. Money is the leading cause of divorce. You should be able to live together on your own, and if you cannot, you should delay marriage. Living with parents, other relatives, or friends is not good, and if you are going to have to, you are better off unmarried for the time being.

5. *One should wait until spiritual matters are settled.* Many a young girl has married a young man to "reform him," only to find that it is a foolish mistake. It is ridiculous to marry a person whose moral and spiritual standards are well below your own.

We have listed five purposes of marriage and five things that should delay marriage. Maturity is one of the requirements for a marriage to be all that it should be. How can you judge whether your maturity level is appropriate for marriage? Here are some good guidelines:

1. When you disagree, do either of you harbor a grudge instead of talking it over with your date or mate?

2. Do you expect to be served instead of showing eagerness to serve your date or mate?

3. Do you hesitate to make real sacrifices?
4. Do you constantly complain when things are not going your way?

If you answered "Yes" to a majority of the questions, it is a good sign you are not yet ready for marriage. If these things happen in your dating life, they will be doubly worse in married life, so tread carefully when considering marriage.

As we close this lesson, allow me to share with you "12 Rules for a Happy Home." Following these rules will help to build a happy and successful marriage:

1. Never both be angry at once. It takes two to argue.
2. Never yell at each other unless the house is on fire.
3. Yield to the wishes of the other, as an exercise in self-discipline if you can't think of a better reason.
4. If you have a choice between making yourself or your mate look good, choose your mate.
5. If you have any criticism, make it lovingly.
6. Never bring up a mistake from the past.
7. Neglect the whole world rather than each other.
8. Never let the day end without saying at least one kind or complimentary thing to your mate.
9. Never meet without an affectionate welcome.
10. Never let the sun go down on an argument unresolved. Never go to sleep mad at each other.
11. When you wrong one another, make sure you have talked it out and asked for forgiveness.
12. Remember, it takes two to make a quarrel. The one with the least sense is the one who would do most of the talking.

Discussion Questions

1. List the characteristics of a potential marriage partner that are most important to you.
2. Do you agree that Christian teenagers should only date other Christians? If not, explain why you think that dating non-Christians is acceptable.
3. Why do you think some young people rush into marriage? How can the conscientious Christian teen avoid rushing into marriage?

Suggested Reading List
Letters TO PHILLIP, Charlie Shedd
Letters TO KAREN, Charlie Shedd
What Every Family Needs, Carl Breechen and Paul Faulkner
Man of Steel and Velvet, Aubrey Andelin
Fascinating Womanhood, Helen Andelin

Lesson 2

"Divorce and Remarriage"

We have already studied God's ideal for dating and making the most of marriage and now we come to a most serious study—Divorce! In my estimation, divorce usually is the result of serious mistakes made in dating or early marriage. Whatever the reason, divorce is spreading like wild-fire through our nation. The divorce rate has increased a whopping 500 percent over the past fifty years. Six decades ago approximately one marriage in eight ended in divorce. Now it's one marriage in two!

There are many "causes" for divorce: money difficulties, sexual problems in the marriage, religious differences, children, sexual immorality (adultery), drunkenness, desertion, mental cruelty, the feminist movement, and that vague term, "incompatibility".

The truth of the matter is that most divorces occur because of *foolish, unwise decisions made during dating or early marriage,* and because of *hard-heartedness.* We do not want you to become a statistic. We want you to have the happy, prosperous, successful marriage God intended for you. Here are some ways to do so:

First, *God intended marriage to be for life, a lifetime contract between you and the person you love.* Marriage is not a temporary arrangement in the sight of God! Too many people today enter into marriage with the idea, "We'll try marriage, and if it doesn't work, we can always get a divorce." That is not true for the Christian! God Himself presides over marriage and intends for it to be a life-time commitment (Matthew 19:3-9, 1 Corinthians 7:10-15, 1 Corinthians 7:39, and Genesis 2:23-24).

Second, *when you marry you make sacred commitments and vows to each other before friends and family and most importantly, before God. You are making a public promise to stay in marriage "until death do us part."* Here is the way the marriage vows are worded. This is what you

Till death do us part.

are committing yourself to follow. This is the promise you are making:

> "Wilt thou have this man (woman) to be thy wedded husband (wife), to live after God's ordinance in the Holy Estate of Matrimony? Wilt thou love him (her), comfort him (her), honor and keep him (her), in sickness and in health; and forsaking all others keep thyself only to him (her), so long as you both shall live?

(Both parties answer these questions)

> "I _____ take thee _____ to be my wedded husband (wife), to have and to hold from this day forward, for better or worse, for richer or poorer, in sickness and in health, to love and to cherish, till death do us part."

(Both parties repeat this vow)

These are holy vows or promises, and they should not be made unless you intend to do everything necessary to live up to them!

Third, *marriage can be broken for only three reasons according to God's Word:*

A. *Death* (Romans 7:2,3). God's desire is that a man and woman remain married until death parts them.

B. *Adultery or Sexual Immorality* (Matthew 19:9). The only time God allows divorce and re-marriage for the innocent party is when his/her marriage partner breaks the marriage bond by adultery. Even in this case, although the Lord permits divorce, He does not require it. The word "fornication" in Matthew 19:9 is the Greek word "porneia," which means whoredom. It seems to imply an ongoing act or continuing adultery. In other words, a persistent course of immorality by a marriage partner would permit the innocent party to divorce and remarry. Even this is abused however by some who would drive a partner to adultery in order to have a "scriptural ground for divorce." God surely frowns on such actions!

C. *Desertion by an unbelieving partner* (1 Corinthians 7:10-15). Some people are so intolerable that no self-respecting Christian can live with them. In this case, God has granted permission for a *separation without remarriage*. This arrangement carries with it the stipulation that the unbeliever not desire to continue in the relationship.

These are the only scriptural reasons for disturbing the marriage contract. It is foolish to speculate that God might allow anything beyond what His Word teaches concerning divorce!

We are as clear and plain spoken on this subject as we know how to be so those not yet married will not rush carelessly to the wedding altar and those married will not consider divorce as a way out of a binding commitment.

"Why is divorce so bad?" someone asks. Let me list a few of the more important reasons:

1. *Divorce shatters the love and happiness both you and God intended for your home.* In fact, in a sense, a messy divorce can be worse psychologically than the death of a mate. With death, the mate is gone and there are usually good memories. In divorce, there is animosity and bitterness. In any case, the tragedy of lost love is always a result of divorce.

2. *If there are children in the family, they are almost always torn between parents and sometimes they suffer the most.* Children need the security, the love, peace and

Never both be angry at once.

contentment of a happy home and a happy marriage. What they least need is what they get in a divorce (custody battles, visitation rights, anger personified, an unhappy atmosphere).

3. *There is usually public suffering for the divorced and their families.* Parents of the divorced often feel that they have failed in some way (whether they have or not). The whisperings and "town talk" is testimony to a failed marriage, and right or wrong, the "talk" always seems to be there. Of course, if you are divorced, most churches are very hesitant about giving you a position of responsibility or leadership.

4. *Financially, divorce can be a disaster.* Most of the time the only one who benefits financially from a divorce

is the lawyer. Women who want to give their children a decent home, a good education, and a high standard of living need to consider very carefully going through a divorce (especially in troublesome economic times). Men who experience divorce also feel the economic strain, either through alimony, child support, loss of business, stress, or remarrying and providing for two households.

5. *Divorce displeases God Almighty.* If this were the only reason, it would be reason enough!

As we noted in lesson one, preventive medicine can go a long way in helping solve the divorce dilemma. The time to avert divorce is before you marry. With this in mind, here are several guidelines to help prevent divorce before marriage:

1. In lesson one, we recommend dating Christians. Don't even consider marrying a non-Christian. Of course, the ideal is to marry not just a Christian, but a good, dedicated one!

2. Carefully examine the family background of the one you want to marry. Families affect character and personality. Often girls imitate their mothers and boys their fathers (even if they don't like to admit it), so check out the mother and father of your desired partner.

3. "Incompatibility" is frequently mentioned as a cause of divorce. Before you marry, be sure you and your partner have mutual interests. Two people who have the same interests are much more likely to get along well.

4. Check out the maturity and "responsibility level" of your partner. There are numerous responsibilities in marriage, and it is foolish to marry an immature

person who isn't ready for obligations, commitments and responsibilities.

5. Be careful about marrying a "hot-head," someone with a terrible temper. This kind of person is difficult to live with.

6. If you marry a drinker, you may spend your life with an alcoholic, and such a marriage is almost unbearable.

7. Be careful about marrying a person who is *always* right about everything. Remember, that means you are *always* going to be wrong about everything!

8. Marry someone who is of the same religious persuasion as yourself. Differences in doctrine can create great friction and tension in a marriage. If you do not marry someone of the same religious persuasion, at least come to some basic agreements about this important subject *before* the marriage.

No doubt many other guidelines should be considered to help decrease the possibility of divorce before marriage, but these are the major ones.

In summary, first, be selective when considering a marriage partner. Second, when you make the commitment, keep it. Third, do everything you can to have a happy marriage. Fourth, when problems arise in marriage, do everything possible to avoid divorce. And finally, if divorce becomes inevitable, be aware of God's laws on divorce and remarriage and do not break them!

God bless you in the critical years that lie ahead as you make decisions that affect a lifetime and an eternity. Choose your course carefully and prayerfully and if we can help, let us know.

Discussion Questions

1. What do you consider to be the most negative result of divorce?
2. What do you consider to be the most important suggestion for preventing divorce *before* marriage?
3. Discuss possible solutions to the ten major causes of divorce mentioned in paragraph two of the lesson.

Suggested Reading List
Divorce and Remarriage, Guy Duty
And I Say Unto You, James Baird
What the Bible Says About Marriage, Divorce, & Remarriage, Olan Hicks

Lesson 3 ——————— —

"What About Abortion?"

Professor L. R. Agnew of the UCLA School of Medicine posed a set of circumstances to his students. "Here is the family history. The father has syphilis, the mother has TB. They have already had four children. The first one is blind, the second one died. The third is deaf, and the fourth has TB.

"The mother is now pregnant with her fifth child. The parents are willing to have an abortion if you decide they should. What do you think?"

A large majority of the students said they would strongly recommend abortion.

"Congratulations!" Agnew told them. "You have just murdered Beethoven!"

Abortion is probably the single most important social issue faced by Americans. Since the U.S. Supreme Court legalized abortion in 1973, more American fetuses have died from abortion than Jews killed in Nazi death camps. Abortion has often been called the "silent holocaust." More human lives were lost to abortion in 1982 than were lost in the atomic bombings of Japan in World War II. Every twenty-four hours, 3,600 American babies are aborted (1981 figures). It is estimated that there are one and a half million abortions in the United States alone each year. Dr. C. Everett Koop, one of the world's leading pediatric surgeons, estimates that Japan has destroyed 50 million pre-born children since abortion was legalized there in 1948.

The statistics are staggering. And it is not just a moral or social issue. It is a Christian issue! Let's use the question method to examine this critical issue of abortion.

What do the scriptures say about the unborn?

David, writing under the inspiration of the Holy Spirit, regarded unborn children as living creatures (Psalm 22:9,10; Psalm 139:13-16). Rebekah was informed by God that He had already made choices concerning the children which were still in her womb (Genesis 25:23). At least two prophets, Isaiah and Jeremiah, were chosen by God while still in their mother's wombs (Isaiah 49:1 and Jeremiah 1:5). "Lo, children are an heritage of the Lord: and the fruit of the womb is his reward" (Psalm 127:3). Now, if God gives life, is it not very dangerous for man to abort that life?

Is the unborn child a person? What does the medical world say?

As the evidence continues to mount, it is clear that the unborn fetus is a living organism. Very early in development, heart beats can be recorded and brain waves detected. The unborn child in the womb responds to pain, kicks a leg, and takes nourishment. According to Dr. Koop, by the sixth week the adrenal gland and the thyroid are functioning. The child's fingerprints are indelibly in place by the twelfth week. Considering the Biblical and medical evidence, the only safe conclusion for a Christian to draw is that an unborn fetus is a person!

How is abortion performed?

This is somewhat gruesome, but those of us who believe that the unborn child is a gift from God and deserves the right to live believe that Christians should know how abortion is performed:

Now, If God gives life is it not very dangerous for man to Abort that life?

A. One method, used during the final three months
    of pregnancy, is the Caesarean Section. It is a
    surgical procedure (very similar to a C-Section live
    birth) where the womb is entered through an
    incision in the wall of the abdomen. The tiny baby
    is removed and allowed to die either through
    neglect or a direct act of aggression.

B. *Dilation and Curettage,* commonly known as *D & C,*
    is the method of abortion most frequently used in
    early pregnancy. The curette, a surgical instru-
    ment, is inserted in the womb through the dilated
    cervix, the natural opening of the womb. The
    abortionist then scrapes the uterus and literally
    cuts the fetus to pieces.

C. Another method of abortion is *salt-poisoning.* Abor-
    tion is performed by inserting a long needle directly
    into the amniotic fluid that surrounds the child.
    The child breathes in and swallows the salt (doesn't
    the baby have to be alive to breathe?), and it slowly
    poisons the baby, burning its skin in the process.
    Some twenty-four hours later, the "mother" will
    deliver a salt-poisoned corpse.

D. The *suction* abortion is also used frequently in early
    pregnancies. This method is similar to the D & C,
    but the difference is that a powerful suction tube
    is inserted through the cervix into the womb. The
    child is torn apart by the suction device and literally
    sucked into a container for disposal.

E. The newest method of abortion is a *chemical*
    technique. Chemicals are injected into the muscle
    of the uterus, causing intense and early con-
    tractions. This really amounts to a chemically
    induced miscarriage.

These are the methods of performing abortion, the realities of the "silent holocaust."

Why do people have abortions?

In view of what we have already seen, how can people choose to abort a baby? There are several reasons, and we will examine them here:

A. *Self-will or selfishness.* The reason many choose abortion is the reason many sin in any instance. They want their own way, and if their own way does not include a child at the present time, abortion is the alternative they seek. In doing so, they are neglecting the rights of the unborn child and the will of God . . . but that is the nature of sin!

B. *Women want control over their own bodies.* Of course, they could have this control by either practicing birth control or by choosing to live differently. But many women say they should have the right to have control over their own bodies. First of all, the unborn child is not really a part of the mother's body. The womb that holds the child is part of the mother's body, but the child is not. The fetus is a biologically separate organism. It has its own genetic code and cellular structure. It has its own brain, its own blood, and its own circulatory and nervous system. Even if the unborn child were a part of its mother's body (and it is not), this would not give the mother the right to destroy the child. We have laws to institutionalize those who abuse themselves physically to prevent them from doing harm to themselves and others.

C. Child abuse or certain poverty is often used as an excuse for abortion. Child abuse has not decreased since the Supreme court decision . . . in fact, it has increased dramatically! And the plea for abortion on the basis of poverty is both foolish and untrue. There are nearly three million couples in the United States who would like to have children and cannot. What a paradox! People who wish to adopt new-born babies must wait years and endure lengthy waiting lists while millions of babies are aborted!

D. Rape and/or incest are presented as valid reasons for abortion. Even if a child is conceived through rape (and studies have shown that it is very rare, the exception not the rule), destroying it will not end the trauma. It does not deter the rapist or punish him in any way. It does not blot out the degradation of the assault (in fact, it probably adds to it). Actually, abortion is the same kind of violence as rape. Certainly, the woman would not have to keep the baby, but in this case, as in all abortion cases, what about the rights of the unborn baby?

These are the primary reasons given for abortion, and the first two listed are overwhelmingly the main reasons.

What can we do about abortion?

A. *We must educate ourselves about abortion.* Far too long we have failed to take a stand against abortion because it is controversial. The more we learn about abortion, the easier it is for a Christian to take a stand against the "silent holocaust."

B. *We must stand for the rights of the unborn child, believing that the "fruit of the womb" is God's heritage.* President Reagan once said, "I notice that everyone who is for abortion has already been born."

C. *We must promote morality and decency.* A majority of abortions are the result of immorality. Perhaps a stronger stand for morality by Christians and churches could help stem the tide.

D. *Let others know how you feel.* The pro-abortionists are active in making their feelings known. There are many ways the concerned Christian can make

"I have a divine right to live."

his/her feelings known (voting, joining pro-life groups, talking to others).
E. *Churches and individual Christians need to help those who have had abortions or who are considering abortion.* Those who have had abortions are often torn by guilt and need good Christian counseling and sympathy. Those considering abortion can be helped by counseling, offering homes for the child, adoption services, etc.

To close this lesson, let me share an article entitled, "The Diary of a Fetus," from *The Capital Voice*, 1981:

"Today I will be slaughtered!

My parents have arranged for me to be murdered. They are paying a man to do this. He is called a doctor.

In the underworld men are hired to kill others. When they are convicted, they are punished by imprisonment or death. But the doctor who has been hired to kill me will never be tried. It is legal. But I am a human being, and have a right to live. God intended that I should be born.

They call me a fetus because I still live in my mother's womb. The word "fetus" means "little one." I am a little human being, and all my systems are working perfectly. In this little room where I live, right under my mother's heart, I have been well taken care of, receiving all the needed nutrients from Mommy's body. I have wanted to be born, just as other children. But my parents do not want me. If I could be born, it might be that someone would adopt me. But my death sentence has already been pronounced, and I must die today.

If I could be born I could bring much happiness to my parents and to all the family. I have the inherited traits and characteristics of my parents, and we could have a lot of fun together.

God has given me a beautiful little body and I do not like the idea of being chopped to pieces, and thrown into the sewer. But I am helpless. If I could only be born and grow up perhaps I could defend myself. But they are going to slaughter me today.

I know I will miss a lot by not being born. I have two beautiful eyes already but they will never see the light of day. Never can I see this big, wonderful world that God created.

I have two ears but I will never hear the sounds of music, laughter and conversation. My little nose will never smell the sweet scent of flowers. I have the sense of taste but I can never enjoy the delicious foods that human beings eat. I have a perfectly formed voice box but I will never be able to speak, sing or laugh.

I am "fearfully and wonderfully made," but today my body will be whittled to pieces. They don't want me. I wonder why?

I will be murdered today. May God have mercy on those who are responsible for killing me.

I am a "fetus," a little one—a little human
being. I have a divine right to live.

It seems to me that we cannot remain neutral on the
issue of abortion. God is not neutral and as His people,
we must not be either.

Discussion Questions

1. What arguments would Satan use to deceive you
   that abortion is acceptable?
2. What do you consider to be the strongest argument
   against abortion?
3. If called upon to counsel a friend who has had an
   abortion, what advice would you give?

Suggested Reading List
Abortion: The Silent Holocaust, John Powell
The Abortion Handbook, Dr. & Mrs. J. C. Wilke
Abortion and the Meaning of Personhood, Clifford Bajema

Lesson 4

"Homosexuality: Alternate Lifestyle or Sin?"

America is facing a serious moral crisis in the homosexual movement. The movement is widespread and broad-based and challenges the moral fabric of our society as it attempts to change our thinking concerning sin and sexuality.

In addition to the moral crisis, there is a medical crisis. AIDS, an acronymn for Acquired Immune Deficiency Syndrome, is spread primarily by homosexual conduct. Homosexuals and bi-sexuals account for approximately 75% of all AIDS cases. As of this printing in early 1988, this deadly virus is 100% fatal. One in one die that contract the disease. Simply put, a diagnosis of AIDS is a death sentence.

Homosexuals claim that they offer an "alternate lifestyle." But, if alternate lifestyle is sin and is opposed to God's will, it must be opposed! Is homosexuality alternate lifestyle, or is it sin? We will attempt to answer that question in this lesson.

What is homosexuality? Simply put, homosexuals are those persons who prefer to have sexual relations with members of their own sex rather than the opposite sex. It is a fact of life that cannot be ignored, for it is

35

estimated that 4-6 percent of the American population is homosexual.

Homosexuals would have us believe they are normal and are really just a third sex . . . but that is not true! God created Adam and Eve—not Adam and Steve! God never created a homosexual, and he condemns this sexual perversion, as we will notice later.

Homosexuals may call themselves ''gay'' but they are not happy. A few years ago the word ''gay'' meant ''fun'' and was utilized by all kinds of people. In recent years, the homosexual community has taken over the

Homosexuals may call themselves "Gay"
but they are not happy.

word. Homosexuals are not really "gay" or happy. Available evidence from social scientists indicate that the homosexual crowd is in a state of despair. The suicide rate among homosexuals is ten to twelve times the rate of heterosexuals. The emotional stress, sense of guilt, loneliness, depression, paranoia, and physical illnesses related to most homosexuals make them anything but "gay!"

What does the Bible teach concerning homosexuality? Both the Old and New Testaments are clear in their condemnation of homosexuality. Homosexuality is not just a sin against one's own body but a blatant violation of the laws of God.

In the Book of Leviticus, Moses listed God's standards for holy living. Leviticus 18:22 clearly states, "Thou shalt not lie with mankind, as with womankind: it is an abomination." Furthermore, it was not only an abomination in the sight of God, but was a sin subject to capital punishment. According to Leviticus 20:13: "If a man also lie with mankind, as he lieth with a woman, both of them have committed an abomination: they shall surely be put to death; their blood shall be upon them."

Jesus' death abolished the ceremonial and civic aspects of the Old Law, so it is wrong to suggest that the death penalty should be imposed on homosexuals. According to the New Testament, homosexuals will be punished by spiritual death. Paul said to the church at Corinth: "Know ye not that the unrighteous shall not inherit the kingdom of God? Be not deceived: neither fornicators, nor idolator, not adulterers, *nor effeminate*, nor abusers of themselves with mankind, nor thieves, not coveteous, nor drunkards, nor revilers, nor extortioners, shall inherit the kingdom of

God" (1 Corinthians 6:9,10). Since the word "effeminate" in the original Greek means "homosexual," this
text indicates that one who chooses homosexuality as
a lifestyle will not inherit eternal life.

Perhaps the most condemning passage concerning
homosexuals in the New Testament is Romans 1:24-28,
where homosexuality is described as "uncleanness,"
"vile affections," "against nature," "shameful" and
the product of "a reprobate mind." By no stretch of the
imagination can a Bible-believer defend the practice of
homosexuality.

Homosexuals often argue their case by saying their
behavior is not their fault. They say homosexuality is
inherited like a big nose or brown eyes. Is homosexuality a genetically related characteristic or a learned
behavior?

The available scholarly evidence indicates that
homosexuality is learned behavior. There is no evidence connecting genetic or hormonal causes with
homosexuality. In an exhaustive, special report on
homosexuality, *Time* magazine concluded, "The only
thing most experts agree on is that homosexuality is
not the result of any kinky gene or hormone predis-
position . . . male and female homosexuals do not
constitute a third sex: biologically they are full men and
women."

If homosexuals are not born that way, the obvious
question is, *What causes homosexuality? Growing Up
Straight*, a book highly endorsed by the National
Institute of Mental Health, says, "Scientific consensus
holds that homosexuality is very largely conditioned
by the environment and childhood and most particularly by parental influence in the home."

Dr. Tim LaHaye, a leading Christian author and lecturer, writes concerning the causes of homosexuality in his book, *What Everyone Should Know About Homosexuality*. Among the causes listed by LaHaye were: (1) Inadequate parental relationships (such as an overly dominant mother or passive father); (2) Permissive childhood training and a lack of discipline;

Inadequate parental relationships.

(3) Insecurity about sexual identity (girls should be taught to be feminine and boys should be taught to be masculine); (4) Improper information about sex during early years (could be caused by promiscuity or the opposite extreme of "All sex is dirty"); and (5) Childhood associates and peer pressure. Of course, sinful lusts and wicked hearts and minds are an obvious cause of homosexuality as well.

Is there a cure for homosexuality? Of course there is, and the cure is the same as for every other sin— obeying Jesus and submitting to Him as Lord! Every reference to homosexuality in the scripture condemn it as a sin (Genesis 19:1-11; Leviticus 18:22; Leviticus 20:13; Deuteronomy 23:17; Judges 19:22-25; Romans 1:24-28; 1 Corinthians 6:9,10; and 1 Timothy 1:9,10). The cure for all sin is Christ! In the case of homosexuality, three things must be done to correct the sin: (1) The homosexual must repent; (2) The homosexual must leave the practice of homosexuality and follow God's will for his life; and (3) The homosexual must be willing to submit to the authority of Jesus as Lord of *all* his life.

This is such an important lesson. Do not underestimate the power of the homosexual community in America. It is a militant force working to gain more acceptance and rights. Their every move influences Christians. We must be informed about homosexuality, concerned about it, and ready to fight it for the following reasons:

1. It is a sin and an abomination against God.
2. Every legal battle the homosexuals win is a loss for Christians.

3. Since homosexuals do not propogate, they must recruit to enjoy their sinful lifestyle . . . and they are recruiting our young people!
4. Homosexual activity is the primary cause of the spread of the fatal AIDS virus.

Those who want to insure their freedom from the deadly AIDS virus and other sexually transmitted diseases can do three things: avoid premarital sexual relations, marry a virgin, and remain faithful to your mate in marriage. It's almost impossible to acquire AIDS, unless, of course, you fool around with a carrier.

Oh, by the way, those three things are what God commands us to do in His Word all along. It pays to follow God's instructions!

Stand against homosexuality! Pray that God will reverse the tide and deliver America from the onslaught of this sin! Do your part to see that homosexuality never becomes an acceptable alternate lifestyle!

Discussion Questions

1. Why are homosexuals definitely not "gay"?
2. How would you raise a child to guard against his/her developing homosexual traits?
3. Why is the homosexual community's fight for more acceptance and rights such a threat to Christianity?

Suggested Reading List
What Everyone Should Know About Homosexuality, Tim LaHaye
As I See Sex Through The Bible, Dr. Robert Pettus
Counseling the Homosexual, Bill Flatt, Dowell Flatt, and Jack P. Lewis

Lesson 5

"The Pollution of Pornography"

Pornography has invaded and polluted our society. Books and magazines which would have been considered filthy and pornographic two decades ago are now called "adult reading." But changing the name does not change the devastation of the results of pornography!

As far as pornography is concerned, the dam has burst and our communities and even our homes are being flooded with filth from magazines, books, television (particularly cable), movies and music (which we will study in a later lesson). It is almost impossible to live in a clean environment. Walk into a store, and you are likely to have vulgar magazines thrust into your face. Turn on the television and you will likely be embarrassed. Full page newspaper ads are explicit in revealing the immorality being shown on the big screen. The pornography industry is a *four billion dollar a year business*.

The promoters of pornography tell us that it is a victim-less crime. That is their biggest lie. Incest, adultery, homosexuality, child abuse, sodomy, violence, rape, and perversion are the common themes of pornography. Ask those who have been the victim of such behavior if pornography is a victim-less crime!

What is pornography? A standard definition of pornography would be "the commercial exploitation of sex, designed to stimulate sexual excitement with special reference to abnormalities and perversions." Beyond that definition, pornography is an attack on the mental, emotional, physical and moral natures of man. It poisons the mind and behavior of the person it controls.

What does the Bible teach concerning pornography? Consider the following passages of scripture:

1. Philippians 4:8: "Finally, brethren, whatsoever things are true, whatsoever things are honest,

Pornography becomes obsessive.

whatsoever things are just, whatsoever things are pure, whatsoever things are lovely, whatsoever things are of good report; if there by any virtue, and if there by any praise, think on these things."

2. 1 Thessalonians 5:22: "Abstain from all appearance of evil."

3. Matthew 5:27,28: "Ye have heard that it was said by them of old time, Thou shalt not commit adultery; But I say unto you, That whosoever looketh on a woman to lust after her hath committed adultery with her already in his heart."

4. Galatians 5:19-21: "The works of the flesh are manifest which are these: fornication, adultery, uncleanness, lasciviousness . . . they which do such things shall not inherit the kingdom of God."

These are four passages which relate directly to pornography, and there are many passages which condemn immorality, adultery, perversion, lust, and filth . . . all the things promoted by pornography.

First, pornography is a threat to the family and marriage. Pornography reduces sex to abnormal perversion rather than the sharing of unselfish, married love. Peter Grosvenor, editor of the *London Daily Express* writes, "The message of hard porn is a fairly constant one: that sex is for self-gratification and kicks; that it has nothing to do with love; that it involves no concern for others. Pornography's whole philosophy (which I might add is Playboy philosophy) is to encourage a variety of relationships rather than any one relationship in depth. Given a free reign, it could spell the beginning of the end for family life and marriage as we know it."

Second, pornography encourages adultery and fornication, glorifying sexual experimentation outside of marriage. Illicit sexual affairs are normal in pornographic books and films. This cannot help but threaten marriage and the family.

Third, pornography dehumanizes both male and female, but particularly females, as mere sex objects. As far as Christian morals are concerned, people are to be loved, but pornography presents people as tools to be *used* for selfish gratification.

Fourth, pornography teaches that the worst kinds of sexual behavior are normal and acceptable. All kinds of perversions are pictured and encouraged in pornography: adultery, homosexuality, sad-masochism (inflicting pain or torture), beastiality, the use of children in immoral acts, rape, etc. It is hardly victimless.

Fifth, pornography affects the community and society. Virtually every study on the effects of pornography have found a close connection between pornography and anti-social action. Many criminals and sex offenders said they behaved the way they did because they were exposed to pornography. Pornography affects a community a number of ways; (A) It becomes an eye-sore offending decent people (what about Christians' rights?); (B) It encourages the immoral; (C) It is backed by organized crime, so the porno industry introduces the community to the criminal underworld; and (D) It makes the local community a more dangerous place to live (increase of rape, violence, etc).

Sixth, pornography becomes obsessive. Those who have been exposed to pornography for extended periods of time say that it is addictive. Pornography becomes an obsession. One man told me that he still can see lewd pictures in his mind that he viewed in a magazine years ago, even though he now is a faithful Christian. Needless to say, it is very difficult to dismiss pornography as "victim-less." The main victim is the user.

Seventh, pornography encourages "mental adultery" (Matthew 5:27,28). Certainly no Bible-believer can deny that this is true!

Eighth, pornography lies about itself, saying that it brings happiness and contentment. Nothing could be further from the truth. In reality, pornography results in guilt, an unwholesome attitude toward sex, improper values, and a dependence upon fantasy rather than reality. It promotes self-gratification and lust, not happiness and contentment. It cannot produce happiness, because it is a blatant violation of everything God wants in His creation.

These are just a few of the evil effects of pornography. A Christian cannot defend it.

What can be done about pornography? Let me suggest several things:

1. *Avoid it! Avoid it!* Do not allow yourself to be exposed to pornography. If you never allow yourself to be exposed to it, you will not have to worry about an ungodly addiction to it (1 Thessalonians 5:22).
2. *Become acquainted with good literature, good television, good movies and good music.* An appreciation of the good will cause you to be repulsed by the vulgar.
3. *Support civil actions to eliminate pornography.* From time to time, groups such as Citizens for Decency Through Law have been successful in having pornography removed from certain local communities. Several towns, including Atlanta, Georgia and Greenville, South Carolina, have had pornographic bookstores closed down. Support any effort to

Avoid pornography.

clean up the filth brought into our communities by the pornographic industries.

4. *For those already polluted by pornography, the only answer is prayer, following the Word of God, and making Jesus Lord of all!* Overcoming the pollution of pornography is not easy, but neither is it impossible when you combine the power of God to deliver from sin with repentance and determination to follow the Lord and His Word.

Pornography is more dangerous than any environmental pollutant. A mental, emotional and moral pollutant, it is a serious threat to decency, morality, and Christianity. It must be opposed. Do your part in opposing it by avoiding it and speaking out against it!

Discussion Questions
1. How would you answer someone who claims that pornography is a victimless crime?
2. Discuss the relationship of pornography to "mental adultery" (Matthew 5:27,28).
3. In what ways can the Christian teenager maintain a clean heart and mind?
4. How would you respond if a friend tried to introduce you to pornography?

Suggested Reading List
See No Evil, T. M. Williams
The Porno Plague, Neil Gallagher

Lesson 6

"Who Is In Charge Here, Anyway?"

Imagine that there were no authority in the home, government, or church. What would result? Anarchy or chaos! We must have authority to have order in our lives.

We have been studying critical issues facing teenagers in the 1980's. Many of these issues have to do with moral principles. The root of many of the moral problems we face today is the topic of this lesson—rebellion against authority.

In at least three areas of a person's life (home, government and church), God has made clear the kind of authority He wants. When children defy, disobey and show disrespect for their parents, they are rebelling against God! When citizens obey only the laws they like or agree with and disobey the rest, they are rebelling against God! When people refuse to submit to the authority of elders in the church, they are rebelling against God!

There is a need for authority. Where does proper authority lie? Who is in charge, and thereby responsible for what happens?

First, *Who is in charge in the home?* There has never been an attack on the home in America like the one we are currently witnessing. Men are rebelling against their responsibilities as head of the home and the family. Women are rebelling against motherhood and against the role God has given them. Young people are rebelling against parents by openly defying them, refusing to obey, and in general, doing as they please.

Authority in the home lies with the parents. Ephesians 6:4 says, "And, ye fathers, provoke not your children to wrath: but bring them up in the nurture and admonition of the Lord." The parent who does not teach his child or teenager respect for authority is doing him a gross injustice. It is weakness on the part of parents to refuse to discipline lovingly and instill respect for proper authority.

Children obey your parents in the lord.

Children and young people in the home are commanded to obey and respect their parent's authority. Ephesians 6:1,2 says, "Children, obey your parents in the Lord: for this right. Honor they father and mother; which is the first commandment with promise." Colossians 3:20 commands, "Children, obey your parents in all things: for this is well pleasing to the Lord." Most young people want fair and reasonable guidelines.

Why do teens rebel against authority in the home? Usually it is because they are caught between childhood and adulthood, wanting to be children still, safe and protected from the outside world, and wanting equally to be adults, rid of the restrictions and containments of childhood. Often a teenager's desire for independence is confused with rebellion against authority. The wise parent will gradually incorporate a sense of independence into the teenager's life.

There are several reasons why teenagers get into trouble with their parents. A few of the most common are:

1. They don't understand what is wrong with an activity or attitude their parents are concerned about. (Example: hitchhiking)
2. They feel their parents are "out-of-date" and haven't kept up with what has changed since they were young. (Example: popular styles.)
3. They don't understand the rules and boundaries that have been given them. Rules should be explained to teenagers.
4. They say, "My parents make a federal case out of everything." Successful is the parent who can point out problems with patience and firmness without "making a federal case out it."

5. They want attention. Often, rebellion against
   parental authority is nothing more than an attempt
   to get the parent's undivided attention.
6. They withdraw as a means of handling disagree-
   ments. Of course, this response must makes things
   worse for everyone concerned.
7. Some teenagers want revenge. They may attempt
   to get even with God. Many have stopped going to
   church to get even with their parents. What a
   shame! Everyone is a loser when this happens.

Parents aren't always right. Any honest parent
would admit that. Nevertheless, authority must lie
somewhere, and God has ordained that in the home,
it lies with parents. Should parents ever be disobeyed
intentionally? Yes, in two instances, both of which
rarely occur: (1) If a parent directly violates the Word
of God, he or she may be disobeyed by the authority
of Acts 5:29, "We ought to obey God rather than men",
and (2) if a parent poses a serious physical threat to
someone in the family, such as severe child abuse.
These instances are uncommon. For the most part,
parents are to be obeyed, even when it appears they
are wrong.

Second, *Who is in charge in government?* It has become
commonplace to disagree with the government on just
about everything. There is nothing wrong with this.
Everyone is entitled to his own opinion. *However, the
right to disagree is not the right to disobey.*

The Roman government in the times of the Apostle
Paul was cruel in many ways. Nevertheless, Paul
encouraged Christians to obey the government: "Let
every soul be subject unto the higher powers. For there
is no power but of God: the powers that be are
ordained of God. Whosoever resisteth the power,

They don't understand what is wrong with an activity or attitude their parents are concerned about.

resisteth the ordinance of God: and they that resist shall receive to themselves damnation. . . . Wherefore ye must needs be subject, not only for wrath, but also for conscience sake" (Romans 13:1, 2, 5).

There is no evidence that early Christians organized movements to defy the Roman government, despite the fact that it was evil, it legalized and encouraged slavery, and it even persecuted and murdered Christians!

God wants us to live by our government's rules and laws, and those who refuse to do so are rebelling against God as well as the government. Once again, there is one exception. When one has to disobey God in order to obey government, the Christian has the right to disobey government (Acts 5:29).

There are several other things the faithful Christian should do for his government:

1. He ought to pray for its leaders (1 Timothy 2:1, 2).
2. He ought to pay proper taxes (Matthew 22:21; Romans 13:7).
3. He ought to act as salt and light, using his influence to bring about better government (Matthew 5:13, 14).

Third, *Who is in charge in the church?* The Lord's church has not escaped the attitude of rebellion which is so prevalent today. Of course, ultimate authority lies in the Word of God as far as spiritual matters are concerned. Anything for which we do not have Biblical authority is forbidden (2 John 7-11).

God saw fit that elders should "shepherd" local churches. Hebrews 13:17 teaches that we are to "obey them that have the rule over you and submit yourselves: for they watch for your souls, as they that must give account, that they may do it with joy, and not with grief: for that is unprofitable for you." When people refuse to obey God's appointed authority in the church, they are rebelling against God!

God made us and He knows what is best for us. He gave us a pattern for authority in the home, government and church, and when we follow His pattern we will be happier! It is the will of God that we submit to God's authority in *all* things and not fall into rebellion. Let's develop a deeper respect for authority and obey it, remembering that rebellion displeases God!

Discussion Questions

1. What situation would make it acceptable for a Christian to disobey government? Be specific, giving possible examples.
2. Why do teenagers often get into trouble with their parents? Which of the reasons mentioned in the lesson are most common?
3. If you were a parent, how would you teach your child respect for authority?

Suggesting Reading List
Young People and Their Lord, Rubel Shelley
A Father Talks to Teenagers, P. D. Wilmeth
How To Be Your Own Selfish Pig, Susan Macawley

Lesson 7

"What Are You Watching?"

What are you watching? If you are the average teenager, you are watching television 6¹/2 hours a day, and you will see 22,000 hours of television by the time you graduate from high school (*U.S. News and World Report*, August 2, 1982). That is roughly twice as many hours as you are in school during twelve years!

Do not misunderstand me! I am not anti-television! Television is one of the most marvelous inventions ever to come from mankind . . . when it is properly used. The problem is that it is often improperly used to promote immorality, violence, wrong values and anti-Christian principles. There is no way a Christian can watch 6¹/2 hours of television a day and keep his mind clean and pure. There are not 6¹/2 hours of decent, wholesome programming during one day!

A Christian is responsible for what he feeds his mind. Many biblical passages indicate that we are responsible for what we see (Psalm 101:3; Philippians 4:8; Matthew 5:27,28; 1 Thessalonians 5:22; 1 Timothy 4:12; Proverbs 23:7; 2 Timothy 2:22). Let's consider three questions about television:

First, *What is positive about television?* Again, I am not anti-television, but as a Christian, I must oppose much of what television promotes. But before we speak out

You will see 22,000 hours of television by the time you graduate from high school.

against the harm resulting from television, let's notice some of the good things television can provide:

a. *Entertainment.* Christians are not opposed to good entertainment or recreation, and television can provide this. There are many forms of good entertainment available on television that the faithful Christian can enjoy with a good conscience (movies that promote good values, most sports, some music, news). As long as television does not violate the moral and ethical standards of God's Word, it is a viable way to spend some leisure time.

b. *Education.* One of the greatest capacities of tele- vision is its ability to educate and inform (as long as you keep in mind that news is often slanted and sometimes permeated with secular humanism).

Many informative or educational programs offered by television are of help in everyday living.

c. *Christianity.* There are several programs and even entire stations devoted to the promotion of Christianity and right living. The possibilities of promoting Christianity on television are virtually unlimited since it is the most influential form of mass media. There is no greater method of getting the gospel to the masses than television!

Second, *what is negative about television?* Neither time nor space will enable us to elaborate on the negative impact television can have, but it is important to notice some of the negative things it provides:

a. *Violence.* The average fifteen year old has witnessed 13,000 deaths and hundreds of crimes and violence on television. Robbery, rape, assault, child abuse, and every conceivable form of murder has been violently portrayed in our living rooms. Is it any wonder that violent crime has experienced a whopping increase since the invention of television?

b. *Crime.* A report prepared by the Judiciary Committee on the U.S. Senate says that "Crime, violence, brutality, sadism and eccentric sex on the television screen must be regarded as a major factor contributing to the rising tide of juvenile delinquency all across the land." This committee found that in one popular 60-minute program, there were 13 killings— nine by shooting, two by stabbing, one by torture, one by smothering. Many crimes are inspired by television plots. The promotion and encouragement of crime by television is a curse on America!

c. *Immorality.* It is difficult to find a television program on the major networks that promotes the family or Christian principles. On the other hand, much of television encourages adultery, riotous living, and in some instances, perversion.

d. *Unrealistic views of life.* The soap operas are particularly guilty in this area. I mean, life really doesn't unfold the way they would have us believe. Neil Postman, a communications professor at New York University says, "TV teaches that all problems can be resolved quickly—within 30 minutes on a sitcom, 30 seconds in a commercial. When that doesn't happen in real life, many people become severely depressed or frustrated." Anything that consistently encourages fantasy rather than reality is a threat to an individual's mental and emotional health.

e. *Wrong heroes.* You are going to have heroes, whether they are good or bad. Christian teenagers who watch all kinds of television run the risk of "idolizing" the wrong kind of heroes, the ones who promote wild, sinful, ungodly lives. During your teenage years, it is vital to have as your heroes those who promote right living.

f. *Less family time.* Anything that takes away from the family being able to spend high quality time together is not good. Television forces the home to become silent, which elevates TV above family sharing. Many parents use the television as a "babysitter," a shameful practice!

g. *Deadening of spiritual values.* Things that were once considered shocking can be watched with indifference. Sin tends to become less sinful as TV dulls the spiritual life.

h. *A lackadaisical attitude.* Even good things become sinful if they divert us from doing what we should

The average fifteen year old has witnessed 13,000 deaths.

do and rob us of a valuable asset—our time.
Television promotes watching rather than doing.
It is usually better to participate in activities rather
than just observing them. I agree with the comment
made in the *Christian Medical Society Journal* a few
years ago: "The primary danger of the television
screen lies not so much in the behavior it produces
as the behavior it prevents."

Now that we have noticed some of the positive and
negative aspects of television, our last question is, *What
should we do about our television viewing habits?* These
suggestions can help the conscientious Christian find
a solution to the television problem:

a. *Control how much television you actually watch.* Six and
    one half hours a day is too much for any teenager.

Limit your TV watching to a few well-selected hours each week.

b. *Avoid watching anything that would teach a different set of moral and spiritual values than is taught in the Word of God.* This takes in a large number of programs which might promote or encourage the things we discussed as being negative concerning television.

c. *Do not neglect priorities or activities for television.* Wholesome activities, homework, family responsibilities and the church should not be neglected for television. This is an unwholesome attitude and can turn you into a "TV addict."

d. *Ask yourself the following question:* Will what I am watching help me or hurt me morally and spiritually? Will what I am watching glorify God or degrade Him? Am I neglecting more important things by watching this program? Am I letting TV become my "idol," just like golden calves were idols in the Old Testament to the heathen? And finally, if Jesus were with me, would He approve of my television viewing habits?

I am not anti-television, but as a Christian I must be opposed to the abuses of television. Think seriously about the positives and negatives of television discussed in this lesson. Pray about this lesson. And pray that God will help you to develop a Christian attitude about what you are watching. God bless you as you strive to serve Him as a Christian teenager!

Discussion Questions

1. What do you think is the most positive attribute of television? What do you think is the most negative attribute of television?

2. Write down the television programs you watch regularly. Do they contain any of the negative elements discussed in the lesson?
3. Discuss some activities that might be of more value than watching television. Why not make a commitment to cut your television viewing in half this week?

Suggested Reading List
Taming the Big Bad Wolves, Joy Witt Berry
How Young People Get Hurt, Robert Taylor

Lesson 8

"What Are You Hearing?"

If you are not listening to the popular music of our day, you may be missing out—missing out on pornography, satanic influence, and appeals to drug abuse, homosexuality, and blatant immorality! Our purpose in this lesson is not to make a blanket condemnation of all popular music (Rock music, Country music, Pop music, etc.). Such a condemnation would be unreasonable. Ultimately, you will choose the kind of music which will influence you, so my desire is to give you a foundation, a Christian perspective from which to make your decision.

Music is everywhere. It has often been called the universal language. We have music in our homes, cars, offices, stores, radios, televisions, restaurants—even in the doctor's office.

Music is powerful, extremely powerful. Music has the capacity to:

1. *Inspire and motivate us.* Christian songs like "Amazing Grace" and "How Great Thou Art" appeal to our emotional spiritual nature. "The National Anthem" and "God Bless America" inspire us to greater patriotism.
2. *Control moods.* Retail stores and restaurants play "mood music," which in a subtle way leaves a

favorable impression on people. And, of course, we know that music is the language of love.

3. *Catch our attention and stick in our minds.* Have you ever found yourself humming the jingle from a television commercial? Music is so powerful in its control over our minds that people who would never drink a drop of beer will find themselves humming or singing a beer commercial!

4. *Call people to action.* It is not accidental that soldiers have gone to war to the tune of music that suggests a cause worth fighting for. School alma maters call the students and alumni of that school to action. And unfortunately, as we will notice later in this lesson, much of today's music is calling people to action as well! But not the kind of action that pleases God.

We could go on citing examples of the way music influences our lives. That influence can be for the good and produce wonderful results . . . or for bad and produce tragic results!

First, let's talk about the people in popular music. In the last lesson, we discussed the importance of having proper heroes and the danger in having the wrong kind of heroes. The truth is, modern music has not been producing many moral role models for Christian teenagers.

The performances and lifestyles of many of the superstars of music indicate the low level of living they advocate. Consider the following examples:

1. *AC/DC's* (which is a sexual euphemism) music deals in sex, violence, and Satanic imagery. Their music suggests that they are involved in Satanic worship. On the cover of their best-selling album, *Highway*

A growing number of modern musicians are involved in Satanic Worship.

to Hell, the band members are dressed in the symbols of Satanism (horns, forked tail, pentagrams, goat heads, and skulls).

2. *Duran Duran's* name is taken from a sex fiend in the cult movie, *Barberalla*. Their music lyrics and video's glory in graphic sex, violence, lesbian affairs, and masturbation.

3. *Madonna*, the queen of contemporary popular music, often performs in lingerie, and has negatively influenced thousands of young teens with her emphasis on sexual revolution and self-expression.

4. *David Lee Roth's* obsession with sex and drugs is legendary. His pride in his sexual conquests led him to purchase film footage of his arrest in Texas for

sexual conduct with a 14-year old girl and put it in his video "Panama." His philosophy is best expressed by his own opening comments to an audience in Detroit, "We are gathered together in celebration of sex, drugs, and rock and roll."

5. *The Beastie Boys* have been banned from several cities for open obscenity on stage and have also been banned by Holiday Inns for cutting holes in the floors of their suites. They have admitted that their chief desire is to be as obnoxious as possible. They have succeeded.

6. *Alice Cooper* claims that he got his name from a spirit that possessed him in a seance. His best-selling albums, entitled *Alice Cooper Goes To Hell* and *Welcome To My Nightmare* contain songs like, "Cold Ethyl," about his love affair with a dead woman's corpse (necrophilia).

To be sure, not everyone in modern music promotes sex, violence, drugs, and satanism . . . but many, if not most, do. We must be careful what type of heroes we promote and enjoy. To support many music stars is, quite simply, blasphemy. Sometimes we are presented with a simple choice: Godly values or Satanic principles!

Second, let's look at the music itself. Sex, drugs, violence, and disrespect for authority are the overwhelmingly dominant themes of popular music (just look at *any* Top Twenty for confirmation). Once again, allow me to list just a sampling of examples:

1. *Jon Bon Jovis*, "Slippery When Wet" album is not about a rain-slickened highway. It is filled with lust and sexual innuendo.

2. The aforementioned *Beastie Boys* raps glorify robbing banks, getting high on drugs, and even killing

people. Perhaps their best known song, "Fight For Your Right To Party" is most characteristic of their rebellious message.

3. *George Michaels'* top hit, "I Want Your Sex" created quite a stir. Even MTV refused to air the video until it was re-edited and featured a taped disclaimer that it may not be appropriate for all viewers. It was not appropriate for any Christian viewers or listeners!

4. Of increasing concern is the reference in rock music to suicide. It has been glorified by several groups:

   a. *Pink Floyd's,* "The Wall" and "Goodbye Cruel World," about isolation from the world and eventual suicide.

   b. *Ozzy Osbourne's,* "Suicide Solution" from the *Blizzard of Oz* album.

   c. *Black Sabbath's,* "Killing Yourself To Live"— ". . .you don't care if you don't see again the light of day. . ."

   d. *AC/DC's,* 'Shoot To Thrill"—". . . put your head up to me, pull the trigger, really do it now, shoot to thrill, way to kill. . ."

5. *KISS's* leader, Gene Simmons, said, "Our music is concerned with sex and little else. In a 1983 Nashville concert, the group screamed to the audience, "Do you care what your parents think of us?" The loud answer from the audience was, "No!" The group asked, "Do you care what your preacher thinks of us?" Again, the loud answer was, "No!" I wish they had asked one more question: "Do you care what Jesus' thinks of us?" I keep wondering what God must think of those professing Christians who idolize this group and others like them.

Drugs and illicit and immoral sex are the predominant themes of popular music today.

What should be the Christian's response to the direction of modern music? Is there anything an honest, conscientious teenager can do? Let me make a few practical suggestions:

1. Realize that there is a problem with much of what is popular music. Be honest, and do not deny the problem. Such music will warp your sense of values about sex, drugs, and heroes.

2. Avoid music which violates the standards of Philippians 4:8: "Finally, brethren, whatsoever things are true, whatsoever things are honest, whatsoever things are just, whatsoever things are pure, whatsoever things are lovely, whatsoever things are of good report, if there be any virtue, and if there be any praise, think on these things."

Avoid music which violates the standards of Philippians 4:8.

3. Alert friends to the negative influences in popular music.

4. Do not support evil and satanic forms of music by listening to them or buying records or concert tickets. It is a shame for Christians to subsidize sin!

5. Be selective in watching musical videos on cable television, particularly MTV. Many are bordering on pornography and are not conducive to pure thinking. Dr. Thomas Radecki, chairman of the National Coalition on Television Violence accused MTV and Warner Communications of featuring "disgusting and destructive violence, gruesome sadism, and hate programming." One thing is certain: as modern technology increases it will be even more important for Christian teenagers to guard what they watch as well as what they hear.

6. Learn to appreciate the good in music. There is nothing wrong with love, romance, adventure and fun in music, so long as it does not include obscenity, vulgarity, pornography, satanism, and violence. So, choose the good, the beautiful, the moral in music.

I hope you will think seriously about what has been discussed in this lesson. We have not condemned all rock and/or country music. We are only concerned with music which is contrary to the Word of God or outside the realm of good taste. If you examine the issue honestly, you will conclude that Christians cannot "seek the Kingdom of God and His righteousness" (Matthew 6:33) and condone most of what is known as modern music.

Think about it. Study the issue. Be honest. Pray about it. The choice is yours . . . but remember, we are all responsible for what we see and hear.

Discussion Questions

1. Do you have any heroes in the music world? If so, who are they? What image would you say they project?
2. Think of the most godly person you know. Would you want to take that person to a concert performed by your favorite musician? If not, why not?
3. Discuss the trend toward satanism in music. Why is this trend so offensive to Christians?

Suggested Reading List
Rock, Bob Larson
Rock Reconsidered, Steve Lawhead
Determining My Values, Clyde Lee Herring

Lesson 9

"What Are You Drinking?"

In a recent Gallup Youth Poll, teenagers named alcohol as one of the three most serious problems facing their generation. These teenagers realized that alcohol abuse is a serious problem. Consider the following facts:

1. Half of all murders and one-third of all suicides in the United States are alcohol related.
2. Alcohol is the number one killer on the highways, a factor in some 30-40,000 deaths and 200,000 injuries each year.
3. In any two year period, drunk drivers kill more Americans than died in the Vietnam war. In a decade, more than a quarter of a million people will die as a result of drunk drivers.
4. The odds are one in two that you will be involved in an automobile accident with a drunk driver sometime during your lifetime.
5. On any given weekend night, it is estimated that one in 10 drivers on the highway is legally drunk.
6. There are at least ten million alcoholics in the United States and millions more problem drinkers (which affects every segment of our society—the home, the work force, the moral fiber of our communities).

The odds are two to one that you will be involved in
an auto accident with a drunk driver.

7. In one hour, at least one American is killed and 20
   injured by a drunk driver!

Alcohol abuse is one of the most serious problems
facing teenagers. Despite the massive drug epidemic
of the past two decades, alcohol remains the most
serious drug problem. It is also our most serious
national health problem.

With all the destruction caused by the abuse of
alcohol, why do Americans permit it to be used? There
are four primary reasons:

First, *the liquor industry is a big business.* Americans
spend nearly 30 billion dollars a year on alcoholic
beverages. Many people are getting rich through the
sale of intoxicating beverages. The government encourages the use of liquor since it claims billions of dollars

each year in federal, state and local taxes from the sale of alcoholic beverages.

Second, *many people enjoy the "highs" that come from drinking.* They are not concerned with what God's Word says, neither are they concerned with the damage caused by alcohol. They will not give up their kicks despite the destruction, tragedy and heartache.

Third, *many people think they can drown their troubles in alcohol.* The irony is their troubles are only magnified by liquor! Using alcohol to dull your problems only hides them temporarily, and when you come back to reality, they have multiplied and are more complicated than ever!

Fourth, *many drinkers are so addicted they cannot stop drinking* (or at least they think they cannot). This is the alcoholic. His entire life is centered around his need for alcohol. One in nine drinkers becomes either an alcoholic or a borderline alcoholic. Their body cannot handle alcohol (the body was not made by God to handle excessive amounts of alcohol).

What does the Bible say about liquor? Consider the following Bible passages:

1. Proverbs 20:1—"Wine is a mocker, strong drink is raging: and whosoever is deceived thereby is not wise."
2. Proverbs 23:20, 21—"Be not among winebibbers: among riotous eaters of flesh: For the drunkard and the glutton shall come to poverty: and drowsiness shall clothe a man with rags."
3. Proverbs 23:31, 32—"Look not thou upon the wine when it is red, when it giveth his color in the cup, when it moveth itself aright. At the last it biteth like a serpent, and stingeth like an adder."

4. Habbukuk 2:15—"Woe unto him that giveth his
   neighbor drink, that putteth the bottle to him, and
   makest him drunken . . ."
5. 1 Corinthians 6:9, 10—"Know ye not that the
   unrighteous shall not inherit the Kingdom of God?
   Be not deceived: neither fornicators, nor idolators,
   nor adulterers, nor effeminate, nor abusers of
   themselves with mankind, nor thieves, nor covetous, *nor drunkards,* nor revilers, nor extortioners,
   shall inherit the kingdom of God."
6. 1 Corinthians 5:11—"But now I have written unto
   you not to keep company, if any man that is called
   a brother be a fornicator, or covetous, or a railer, *or
   a drunkard,* or an extortioner; with such an one no
   not to eat."

These are just a few of the many passages of
scripture which condemn the abuse of alcoholic
beverages. I would recommend complete abstinence
from alcohol. That is the safe and sure position. There
are at least three god reasons for it:

First, *alcohol is harmful to the physical body, and the body
is the temple of God* (1 Corinthians 3:16, 17; 6:19, 20).
Medical research has conclusively shown that alcohol
causes both immediate and long-range damage to the
body. Brain cells die when alcohol is taken into the
blood stream. The heart, the liver, and the kidneys are
adversely affected by alcohol. Alcohol also causes
spiritual and emotional abuse to the human system.

Second, *the role of alcohol in our modern society makes
it difficult, if not impossible, for a Christian to defend.*
Alcohol is the friend of such sins as revellings,
drunkenness, lasciviousness, murders, and strife. The
liquor industry deals in death, misery, addiction,
destruction of innocent lives and personal tragedy.

Paul commanded us to "Abstain from all appearance of evil" (1 Thessalonians 5:22). Can anyone argue that alcohol use is abstaining from evil? Can we find good, uplifting, Christ-honoring associations with alcohol? Does it glorify God?

Third, *a Christian should not drink because of his influence.* Romans 14:21 plainly states, "It is good to neither eat flesh, nor to drink wine, nor anything whereby thy brother stumbleth, or is offended, or is made weak." There was never a beer joint that didn't turn out drunkards. Christians who drink are condoning the use of alcohol and will turn out people under their sphere of influence who will drink also.

There are many other good reasons for abstaining from alcohol, but these are the primary ones.

This brings us to some questions often asked about the use of alcoholic beverages in the Bible. First, someone asks, "Didn't Jesus turn water into wine?" Well, the Greek says that he turned water into *oinos*, a generic term that could speak of either fermented wine or non-fermented fruit juice. If you interpret that it was fermented, intoxicating wine that Jesus made, then you have Him contradicting and refuting the many passages of scripture which condemn intoxicating beverages. It seems much more reasonable to assume that our Lord made *oinos,* a non-toxicating wine at the marriage feast at Cana in John 2.

Someone else asks, "Didn't Paul tell Timothy to drink wine for his stomach's sake?" Yes, he did, but unquestionably Paul was referring to the use of a small amount of wine for medicinal purposes, in this case, a stomach ailment. Do not try to defend the use of alcohol for personal pleasure with the argument that it may be used for medicinal purposes. That is not an honest approach!

What can you do about the problem of alcohol abuse? Let me suggest several things:

1. *Get the facts about alcohol and make an intelligent decision about the use of it.* In what way does the drinker profit mentally, emotionally, physically or spiritually from the use of alcohol? The truth is that he does not profit at all from using alcohol, but in a number of ways he loses. It is not likely that you will avoid alcohol because your parents or I encourage you to do so. Eventually, you will make your own decision, so get *all* the facts and consider them carefully and prayerfully.

"Be not among winebibbers."

2. *Don't take the artificial way out of your problems.* Learn to deal with the problems that made you want to turn to alcohol. Deal with the problem itself, whether it be peer pressure, family problems, or a lack of self esteem.
3. *Allow others to help if you are faced with an alcohol problem.* Seek out someone who can give you encouragement and counseling. Teachers, church leaders, parents, Christian friends are usually willing to help in any way they can. Allow them to help you!
4. *Study everything the Bible says about alcohol and its abuse.* Such an honest and objective study should convince you that abstinence is the best policy.

This is a serious problem. Most of us know those whose lives have been shattered by the use of alcoholic beverages. The most you can say or do as a Christian teenager to oppose the evils of alcohol is too little, but you can and should do your part. If you do your part, you will be happier and God will be pleased.

Discussion Questions
1. If you lost a loved one or a friend in a drunk driving accident, how would you feel? Would it increase your outrage against this problem?
2. Can a person really "drown their troubles" in a bottle of alcohol? If not, why not?
3. Defend the position of complete abstinence from alcohol. Or, if you are of the disposition that drinking is acceptable for a Christian, defend your position.

Suggested Reading List
Social Drinking and the Christian, Don Humphrey
The Bible and Strong Drink, Howard Winters
The Bible, Saint, and Liquor Industry, Jim McGuiggan

Lesson 10 ———————————————

"What Are You Smoking?"

Cigarette smoking is so widespread that it must be an innocent pastime, right? Wrong! Just because approximately 42 percent of American men, and 32 percent of American women smoke does not make it right or safe. In fact, thousands of habitual smokers pay a heavy price for their smoking each year, as they die from heart disease, lung cancer and other respiratory ailments.

If smoking is innocent, why did the government remove advertisements for cigarettes from television a little over a decade ago? If smoking is innocent, why does our government require that all cigarette packages contain the words, "Warning: Cigarette smoking may be hazardous to your health." If smoking is innocent, why is the incident of lung cancer (unquestionably caused by smoking) 1,000 percent more frequent among smokers than non-smokers? Smoking is not an innocent pastime. It is a serious health threat!

Beyond the fact that smoking is a threat to health, our concern is whether or not smoking presents a problem to the Christian. Let's look at a number of ways smoking seems incompatible with Christianity:

First, *Jesus is our perfect example, and I do not believe he would smoke.* I cannot imagine Jesus smoking. For Him to do so, knowing how hazardous it is to our health, would be a gross inconsistency.

Second, *smoking is harmful and destructive to your God-given body*. Smoking defiles the body, which is the temple of the Holy Spirit. Consider the words of Paul in 1 Corinthians 3:16, 17; "Know ye not that ye are the temple of God, and that the Spirit of God dwelleth in you? If any man defile the temple of God, him shall God destroy; for the temple of God is holy, which temple ye are."

Paul further stated in 1 Corinthians 6:19, 20: "What? Know ye not that your body is the temple of the Holy Ghost which is in you, which ye have of God, and ye are not your own? For ye are bought with a price: therefore glorify God in your body, and in your spirit, which are God's." Smoking is harmful to the body. As far back as 1964, Surgeon General Luther Terry's Advisory Committee report on smoking came to the overwhelming conclusion that:

a. Cigarette smoking causes lung cancer.
b. Cigarette smoking is the most important cause of chronic bronchitis: it also increases the risk of death from pulmonary emphysema. (Have you heard someone fighting for every breath?)
c. Cigarette smoking greatly reduces lung function. Breathlessness is far more prevalent among smokers than non-smokers.
d. Cigarette smoking is a "significant factor" in causing cancer of the larynx in men, and there is some connection between cigarette smoking and cancer of the esophagus and of the urinary bladder.
e. Cigarette smokers have a 70 percent higher death rate from coronary heart disease than non-smoker.

Smoking is habit forming.

f. Heavy smokers pay with 34.6 minutes of life for each cigarette smoked; the pack-a-day smoker pays with 11.5 minutes for each pack smoked.

Since this exhaustive report of nearly 20 years ago, research has continued to find smoking hazardous. The body which is being destroyed bit by bit through smoking is the temple of the Holy Spirit! This "slow suicide," as smoking has often been called, is defiling the temple of God.

Third, *smoking hinders Christian influence.* If your example leads others to do what they think is wrong, or if you cause them to be discouraged and lose confidence in Christianity, you have sinned (1 Corinthians 8:9-13; Romans 14:21). Parents, church leaders and friends have led many teenagers astray by their bad example in smoking. There is nothing in the Bible that justifies a double standard of morals. If smoking is wrong, it is wrong for everybody. If smoking is harmless and right, it is right for everybody! Christians are responsible for their influence. If they have wounded the weak conscience of a brother or sister in Christ, they have sinned with their influence.

Fourth, *smoking is habit-forming and results in a lack of self control.* I have heard of people warned by their doctor that if they continued smoking they would soon die. They continued smoking, and they died! They could not give it up, it was so addictive, so habit-forming! We are to "keep our body, and bring it into subjection" (1 Corinthians 9:27). When one is such a slave to nicotine that he cannot stop smoking, he is hardly bringing his body under subjection. In fact, to the contrary, his body has brought him under subjection to its desires!

Fifth, *smoking is offensive to non-smokers.* We are to "love one another" and "prefer one another" (Romans 12:9, 10). It is sad to see a Christian trying to avoid the harmful effects of smoking having it thrust into his face by another Christian. To the non-smoker, smoke is nauseating. Christian love and concern for others demands that we be considerate and not force things on them that they are trying to avoid.

Sixth, *smoking has caused grief and suffering for many people.* Have you visited a friend or a loved one who is dying of cancer? Have you seen the cancer-eaten victims of smoking? Have you heard a cancer victim gasp for every breath? Have you seen the hurt and grief

on the faces of loved ones as they give up precious
loved ones to death when the primary cause was
smoking? I have witnessed these scenes many times,
and it is always painful. In almost every case, it could
have been avoided.

Why do people smoke? Most beginning smokers are
young people. The United States Department of
Health, Education and Welfare estimates that approximately one million teenagers begin smoking each year.
At least 80 percent of American teenagers are smoking
or have tried smoking. Why?

First, parents have an important influence on
whether or not their children start smoking. The child
learns about adult behavior through his parents, and
he may come to associate smoking with being mature
like his father or mother. An older brother or sister
may have the same effect on a younger child.

Second, many young people start smoking even
though their parents abstain and may be opposed, due
to peer pressure. Teenagers often try their first
cigarette at the urging of friends. Smoking may be an
accepted and admired habit within the teenagers' circle
of friends, and if he/she does not participate, he may
feel left out. He may be called "chicken," or worse.

Third, teenagers may see smoking as a symbol of
their independence, a sign of adulthood. Some young
people start smoking to appear grown up, mature and
sophisticated (cigarette advertisements encourage this
reaction). The male smoker is portrayed as tough, the
female smoker as liberated. Actually, the smoker
becomes weak, unable to control his own destiny and
enslaved to nicotine!

What can the Christian do about smoking? Let me
suggest some things:

Smoking is harmful.

1. *Don't start smoking!* If you are one of the fortunate teens who has never started smoking, hurray for you, and don't start! There is no good reason for you to start smoking. There are many reasons why you should not.
2. *If you have started smoking, stop immediately!* Do not taper off gradually, stop completely! This will be one of the hardest things you have ever tried to do, but it will be worth the effort in the long run.
3. *Do not linger around where people smoke.* Stay out of situations where you may be tempted to smoke. "Abstain from all appearance of evil" (1 Thessalonians 5:22).
4. *Pray for strength to overcome the habit.* God can and will give grace for every temptation. I know one person who quit smoking by successfully claiming the promise of 1 Corinthians 10:13, "There hath no temptation taken you but such as is common to

man: but God is faithful, who will not suffer you to be tempted above that ye are able; but will with the temptation also make a way to escape, that ye may be able to bear it." Pray!

5. *Since smoking is a habit-forming, addictive thing, realize that you must replace it with something else.* Every time you want a cigarette, reach for a piece of gum, or candy, or fruit. Substitute other motions for smoking, and fill your thoughts and taste with something else. Thousands of people have stopped smoking this way.

6. *Focus on the positive results stopping smoking will bring you.* Food tastes better. The bad taste in the mouth disappears. Smokers' breath is gone. Self-control gives you pride and respect. You will improve your health. And most important, you will please God Almighty!

The evidence presented in this lesson from both the Christian viewpoint and the medical world is sufficient to show that smoking is harmful physically, emotionally and spiritually. Weigh the evidence prayerfully and avoid the addictive, bad habit of smoking.

Discussion Questions

1. Which of the six ways smoking seems incompatible with Christianity do you consider most valid?
2. How would you answer the question, "Why do people smoke?"
3. Contrast the positives and negatives of smoking. Write them down on a sheet of paper. Which side wins?

Suggested Reading List
Health, John LaPlace
Dare To Be Different, Fred Hartley
Tobacco and the Christian, Eugene Hibbett

Lesson 11 ———————————

"What About Drugs?"

We are living in a drug culture. A literal epidemic has broken out. If you are like most teenagers, you've probably read or heard about drug abuse and you may have seen some of your friends when they were high on drugs. It is not a pretty sight!

Perhaps you have heard some of the horror stories concerning the use of drugs. Consider the tragedy of the Art Linkletter family when their beautiful and talented 21 year old daughter took a hard drug and, thinking she could fly, stepped out a fourth-story window to her death. Multiplied thousands of families have experienced similar tragedies because of drug abuse.

One survey indicated that 65 percent of high school seniors nation-wide have used an illegal drug at some time or another in their lives. That is a startling statistic, but statistics about other people do not mean much to most of us. People do not stop using drugs just because they read horror stories of cold statistics. The drug problem and its solution isn't that simple.

When we discuss drug abuse in this lesson, we are referring to any non-prescribed substance that alters the function of the human mind and brings about a change of personality and behavior. We are not talking about aspirins, cold tablets, or prescription drugs. The kind of drugs which create problems are those used either to "turn you on" or "calm you down." The following drugs would fit into this category: cocaine, marijuana, barbiturates, tranquilizers, amphetamines, LSD, PSP, angel dust, heroin, methadone, morphine, and opium.

Two questions stand out in our discussion of drug abuse: First, considering all the negative consequences, why do teenagers start taking drugs in the first place? Second, what can teenagers do about drugs?

There are several reasons why teenagers involve themselves with drugs (none of them are valid):

Don't ruin your future with Drugs.

1. *Many start using drugs because of the example of their parents.* Some time ago a cartoon appeared in the *Wall Street Journal.* A distressed teenager is sitting at a bar and tells the bartender, "I'm trying to solve my problems like an adult." The cartoon was more tragic than funny. If your parents or other adults you know have turned to drugs or alcohol to "solve" their problems or pressures, you may follow their example and turn to the same things. Nearly 60 percent of the children of alcoholics are problem-drinkers themselves, and probably a similar percentage would be true of the children of drug abusers.

2. *Pressure from other teenagers causes many teens to experiment with drugs.* A survey of high school students indicated that most teens who had tried drugs did so for the first time because of pressure from their friends. Once the teen began using drugs regularly, he or she would be likely to introduce others to drugs. It is a vicious cycle! Peer pressure is difficult to deal with, since if you say "No" your friends might criticize you or make fun of you. You must resist. You will be glad you did! For many teens the first pill begins a long, treacherous slide into addiction . . . a slide they did not predict or want, a slide that ruins their life!

3. *Some teens use drugs to escape from unpleasant experiences.* Perhaps they are troubled with disappointment, guilt, boredom, loneliness, the fear of failure, the fear of rejection, so they take drugs, particularly "uppers" or "downers," hoping to escape from their problems. The escape is only temporary. When the drug wears off the problem

is still there and may be even greater because dependency or addiction has begun.

4. *Some teens use drugs as a form of protest or rebellion.* Much of our drug problem had its roots in the protest movement of the late 1960's and early 1970's. Drugs became a way to get back at those with whom we disagree (parents, teachers, friends, government, and school). In one sense this accomplishes the purpose, since those we intend to hurt are frustrated and upset. But who is the real loser? It is the protester, who ruins his life and future . . . if he is still alive.

Every young person should know the *full* story on drugs, for even a single dose can destroy his life. Drugs are harmful both physically and mentally.

There are some ways to deal with drug problems, which brings us to our second question: What can teenagers do about drugs?:

1. *Get the facts about drugs and make an intelligent decision about them.* Avoiding drugs is the only logical solution. Use your brain! You are not likely to avoid drugs because your parents, preacher, or friends encourage you to do so. Ultimately, you will make your own decision, so be wise and mature. Get *all* the facts, and consider them carefully.

2. *Learn to deal with problems that might cause you to take drugs.* You cannot drift above your problems in a state of euphoria. Eventually you must come down, and the fall will be great! Deal with the problem itself. Using drugs to dull your problems only hides them for the moment. When you come back to reality, they will have multiplied and become more complicated than ever!

3. *Be aware of the symptoms of drug abuse so you might help friends who need your support.* The following signs are strong indicators of drug abuse or addiction:

a. Sudden mood shifts, from normal to angry or highly provocative, can be triggered by drug abuse.

b. Slurred speech.

c. New habits like the wearing of sunglasses (to hide dilated pupils) or wearing long sleeves all the time (to cover needle marks).

Get the facts about drugs.

d. Repeated attempts to borrow money (to be used
   for buying drugs). The very best thing a friend can
   do for someone who is using drugs is to encourage
   them to get help.
4. *Make up your mind that you will not sacrifice your health
   and future for drugs.* Arthur Schopenhauer, the
   German philosopher, wisely wrote: "The greatest
   mistake any person can make is to sacrifice health
   for any other advantage." Our bodies are the temple
   of the Holy Spirit (1 Corinthians 6:12-19) and are to
   be presented to the Lord as a living sacrifice
   (Romans 12:1, 2). Once your health is gone, it can
   never be fully regained.
5. *Turn to God!* This is not a trite and simplistic answer.
   Christians are less likely to take drugs. Drug abuse
   is most common among those who have few
   spiritual values. Jesus Christ gives meaning to life
   and help and peace to those who are willing to let
   Him be in control.

Drug abuse is a serious problem. The best advice is
to avoid drugs completely! If you get involved with
drugs, seek competent help as quickly as possible. If
you know someone involved with drugs, encourage
them gently and lovingly to get help.

If you must get high on something, get high on
God. He will never let you down! He is the only
dependency you can trust!

Discussion Questions
1. If you know someone on drugs, why do you think
   they are involved with them? How would you go
   about trying to help them?

2. Discuss some of the ways drugs destroy a person physically and mentally.
3. What would you do if someone approached you about taking drugs? Are there specific people in your life that you could turn to for help?

Suggested Reading List
The Great Marijuana Debate, Barrett and DeHoff
Drugs and Drinking: All American Cop-Out, Jay Strack
Five Cries of Youth, Merton Strommon

Lesson 12

"What About Peer Pressure?"

Over the past few years, I have seen young people do things they never planned to do, things they really did not want to do, things they knew would wind up hurting them. Why? Because of peer pressure. I have watched a number of teenagers reject the gospel or not be active in church activities. Why? Because they were fearful of what their peers might say or think.

Peer pressure is a powerful force teenagers face when making decisions. What is peer pressure? Basically, it is three things:

1. Peer pressure is going along with the crowd because it's the popular thing to do in order to be accepted.
2. Peer pressure is feeling pressured to do things you know are wrong. Decisions are not based upon right and wrong, but upon the "majority opinion." This kind of peer pressure says, "Everybody is doing it." Decisions are based upon what "everybody" is doing, not what is right or wrong.
3. Peer pressure is not being sure whether or not you fit in with the crowd. This kind of peer pressure can cause a teenager to withdraw and become a loner. The teenager may not be a misfit at all, but the crowd made him feel like one, so he is pressured into an unhealthy withdrawal.

Why does peer pressure have such control over many teenagers? Teenagers, like most people, have a basic need to be accepted, to be popular. There is nothing wrong with being popular, as long as one does not have to pay *any* price for it.

What kind of price tag have you put on popularity? If you can answer that question, you can determine the degree you will be influenced by peer pressure. Answer these three questions honestly:

1. *With whom do you want to be popular?* You cannot be popular with everyone, so you must make a choice about the crowd you want to be popular with—those who claim Christ or those who deny Him by their lives.

2. *What kind of popularity do you want?* Make up your mind which crowd you want to be a part of—the drug crowd, the rebellious crowd, the "do-your-own-thing" crowd . . . or the Christian crowd. Sometimes you have to make a choice because the two simply do not mix! When determining which crowd you want to be a part of, ask yourself these questions: "How do their standards match up to mine? How much am I willing to sacrifice or compromise in order to be accepted? What price will I pay for being a part of this crowd?"

3. *Why do I want to be popular?* Some teenagers go along with the crowd even when they don't want to, because they are afraid of going it alone. Granted, it is easier to just be one of the gang, but that is not the healthiest response emotionally or spiritually.

Do not misunderstand me. There is nothing wrong with being popular so long as you do not have to pay a terrible price. Does the Bible have anything to say about peer pressure as it relates to popularity? Consider the following scriptures:

1. Romans 12:1,2: "I beseech you therefore brethren, by the mercies of God that you present your bodies a living sacrifice, holy, acceptable unto God, which is your reasonable service. *And be not conformed to this world* (a modern paraphrase says, "Do not let the world squeeze you into its mold"): but be ye transformed by the renewing of your mind, that ye may prove what is that good, and acceptable, and perfect will of God."

2. James 4:4: "Ye adulterers and adulteresses, know ye not that the friendship with the world is enmity with God? Whosoever therefore will be a friend of the world is the enemy of God."

3. 1 John 2:15: "Love not the world, neither the things that are in the world. If any man love the world, the love of the Father is not in him."

4. Proverbs 1:10,15: "My son, if sinners entice thee, consent thou not . . . My son, walk not in the ways with them: refrain thy foot from their path."

God has something to say about the price of popularity. Popularity is fine and good and can even be used by God to bring about good. Popularity is fine as long as you sway the crowd for the right and do not let the crowd sway you to the wrong.

Peer pressure is hard to resist. It is easy to give in and join the crowd. On the other hand, it isn't easy to say, "No", when others make you feel like an oddball, "stupid," or "chicken." Why do some people put such pressure on those who say, "No?" They are weak and have trouble accepting those who are strong enough to resist! They have sold out and gone along with the crowd, losing their individuality and uniqueness, and they hate to see people who do not buckle under pressure!

When the pressure builds up, resist the temptation to give in. People make all sorts of excuses for giving in to peer pressure:

1. "Since everybody is doing it, it must be okay."
2. "Nobody would know if I gave in just this once."
3. "I'll try it once just to get them off my back."
4. "I need to try it to know if it's wrong."

I hope you will fight the excuses to give in and stick to your guns. When you do give in, you lose. You lose your principles, your uniqueness, your self-respect, your freedom of choice and maybe a lot more!

Many times we have heard Christian teenagers who got into trouble say, "My friends got me into it." My heart goes out to young people, because the Devil has used peer pressure to ruin many of their lives. But, you can have victory over peer pressure! Let me give you

Learn to say no and mean it.

five practical suggestions for dealing with peer pressure:

1. *Resist it with all your might!* Be yourself. Be what God intended you to be and not what others want you to be, which is weak! Use your mind to resist what you know is wrong, just as others have used their minds to give in to wrong. Resistance involves relying on others (youth group, minister, parents, and Christian friends, as well as relying on God to give you the grace to withstand peer pressure (1 Corinthians 10:13).

2. *Avoid peer pressure by not putting yourself into tempting situations.* If you have trouble avoiding temptation (and most of us do), then whenever you can, avoid situations that would tempt you. If some people put you under special pressure, it may be best to steer clear of them and their influence. Remember, 1 Thessalonians 5:22 says, "Abstain from all appearance of evil." That's good advice in dealing with peer pressure!

3. *When peer pressure to do wrong is inevitable, learn to say "No" and mean it.* Someone will always try to influence you to do wrong. The best way to let people know that you are not interested is to say, "No", and then walk away. Don't linger and let temptation have another chance at you.

4. *Make up your mind to do right, even if no one else does.* You cannot go wrong if you do right. Paul knew this feeling. He said to Timothy, "At my first answer no man stood with me, but all men forsook me" (2 Timothy 4:16). Even if you have to go it alone for awhile, you can be sure the Lord will bless you for your stand for righteousness.

5. *Have the right kind of friends or don't have any friends at all.* One would be better off with no friends than with the wrong kind of friends. Our friends have a way of telling on us. If I could spend time with your best friend, I could tell how you were living. "Birds of a feather flock together." Remember the admonition of 1 Corinthians 15:33: "Be not deceived, evil company corrupts good manners."

You can deal with peer pressure and triumph over it, but you must make up your mind to do so. It will not be easy. But the rewards will be great! May God give you the courage not to go along with the crowd, but to go with Jesus Christ, your Saviour and Lord!

Discussion Questions

1. What's something you feel pressured about? Are there certain people who pressure you?
2. Discuss the attributes of acceptable popularity. Discuss the high price some pay for popularity.
3. How can you learn to say, "No" and make it so clear that everyone understands?

Suggested Reading List
Preparing For Adolescence, James Dobson
Growing Pains, Fred Hartley
How To Be A Christian In An Unchristian World, Fritz Ridenour

Lesson 13

"Please, Don't Foul Up Your Future!"

The final lesson in this series on the critical issues facing teenagers today is a plea . . . an honest, heartfelt plea, that you will enjoy your teenage years, but that you will not make foolish, unwise decisions that may cripple your future happiness.

So many young adults look back at their teen years and say, "If only I had done this or that differently . . ." Their whole future has been fouled up by seemingly innocent decisions made during their teen years. We do not want this to happen to you. We want you to enjoy a clean, wholesome, fun teenage life, but we also want you to make decisions and commitments that will insure that you have a productive and happy future.

God wants you to be happy. He intended for His people to live in "fullness of joy" (1 John 1:4). But many people have confused this joy, this sense of inner happiness, with pleasure. In doing so, they can never find contentment.

The word "pleasure" comes from the word "please," and it is derived from those things which please the senses (sight, smell, touch, hearing, etc.). There are good pleasures (the sunshine, rain, flowers, food, laughter, recreation, and hobbies) that enrich life, but they bring pleasure rather than the inner happiness the Bible speaks about. There are also bad pleasures (immorality, unwholesome entertainment, alcohol, and riotous living) which may bring a moment of temporary pleasure, but ultimately bring us harm rather than good.

Happiness is different from pleasure, in that pleasure comes from those things that please the senses, while happiness can result even from unpleasant experiences. Jesus spoke of the mother who knows the pain of childbirth, yet joy at the same time (John 16:21). A father will work long, hard, tedious hours, enduring many hardships, for the joy of providing for those he loves. The apostle Paul, while in prison, nevertheless said, "Not that I speak in regard to need, for I have learned in whatever state I am, to be content"

What would Jesus do...

(Philippians 4:11). Any person who has a high goal and is dedicated to reaching that goal will know struggle and opposition, but he will also experience great joy, the joy of accomplishment and fulfillment when the goal has been reached. Inner happiness is different from mere pleasure.

How can we have this inner happiness, this fullness of joy? It can only be obtained by following eternal laws. There are spiritual laws governing happiness, just as surely as there are natural laws governing the universe. When people experience deep inner contentment, it is because they are following the spiritual laws upon which happiness is based. How do we get this kind of inner happiness?:

1. *By being obedient to God.* No one can know true inner peace and joy without obeying God and His commands. He made us and He knows what is best for us and what will make us happy and fulfilled. Unless we obey God, we will always have an emptiness, a vacuum, a fear of death and the future. How can we be happy if we know we may be eternally lost? Obedience to the Creator is a prerequisite to true happiness!

2. *By fellowshipping with God.* Not only must we be obedient to God, but we must fellowship with Him. A modern writer once said: "Inside each person is a God-shaped vacuum, and only God can fill that vacuum." If there is emptiness in your life, it can be filled, but only God can fill it! All other searches for fulfillment are fruitless and vain.

3. *By righteous living.* A sinful person is so far removed from real happiness they are not familiar with the feeling. Sinfulness leads to depression, nervousness, seemingly insurmountable problems, and a

What does the Bible say.

feeling of worthlessness. The happy people are those who are serving God, using their talents unselfishly, are kind and responsible and have high moral standards.

A great speaker once said, "One's happiness will not be determined by how happy he is on his happiest day, but by how happy he is on his saddest day. It is not the height of the mountains but the height of the valleys that determines joy and happiness." If you can learn to develop deep inner happiness, you have a bright future!

Every day you make decisions that will determine your destiny on earth and in eternity. How can you make wise decisions? Here are some questions to ask yourself about decision-making:

1. *What does the Bible say?* If God's Word gives
   direction, that should settle the issue for the
   Christian. Of course, some activities are always
   wrong, regardless of the situation. For example,
   there is never a right time to lie or murder.
2. *What does the world think?* Because of his influence,
   a Christian has a responsibility toward other people.
   It is important what they think, particularly if my
   participation in activity causes another person to
   stumble spiritually (1 Corinthians 8:13; Romans
   14:21).
3. *Will my decision glorify God?* The apostle Paul says
   in 1 Corinthians 10:31, "Whether, then, you eat or
   drink or whatever you do, do all to the glory of
   God." In Colossians 3:17, Paul teaches again, "And

Happiness is different than pleasure.

whatever you do in word or deed, do all in the name of the Lord Jesus, giving thanks through Him to God the Father." We are God's mirrors to reflect Jesus to the world. We are Christ's ambassadors to the world (2 Corinthians 5:20).

4. *What will be the results?* Sometimes a thing may appear fine at the moment, but further investigation, it can be seen to be harmful in the future. Evidently this is what Solomon had in mind when he penned the words, "There is a way that seemeth right unto a man, but the end thereof are the ways of death" (Proverbs 16:25).

5. *Can I ask God's blessing on this matter?* If an activity is right and proper, you could ask God's blessing on it. If you hesitate to ask God's blessing, you should hesitate to participate in the activity!

6. *What would Jesus do?* This is the acid test in decision-making.

By considering these questions honestly and maturely, you can be sure of making wise decisions most of the time. These questions serve as good Biblical and spiritual criteria for making decisions about activities that will affect your future. Try them as you make decisions, and see how they influence your decision-making process!

We have tried to address the issues of the day that are of pressing interest to you, the issues that are affecting your life. We want to give you a Biblical perspective on the critical issues facing teenagers.

You have so much of life ahead of you. Make the most of it! Live for God! Allow Him to control your life, and you will have a glorious future both in this life and in eternity! May God bless you as you make these critical decisions that will determine your destiny!

**May God give you the courage not
to go along with the crowd.**

Discussion Questions
1. Where do you think you will be, spiritually and
   morally speaking, ten years from now?
2. Discuss your views on real inner happiness. Discuss
   the difference between happiness and pleasure.
   When are you most secure?
3. Determine the next time you are faced with a moral
   decision to apply the six-question test mentioned

in the lesson. Discuss moral issues taught in this series of lessons and apply the six-question test to them.

Suggested Reading List
Expect to Win, Bill Glass
Career Decision Making, Jim Riddell and Melvin Whitehurst
Christian Living Is For Real, Tim Walker